POP PIANO HITS

SIMPLE ARRANGEMENTS FOR STUDENTS OF ALL AGES

Feel It Still, Rewrite the Stars & More Hot Singles

ISBN: 978-1-5400-2947-8

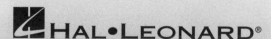

Visit Hal Leonard Online at
www.halleonard.com

Contact Us:
Hal Leonard
7777 West Bluemound Road
Milwaukee, WI 53213
Email: info@halleonard.com

In Europe contact:
Hal Leonard Europe Limited
Distribution Centre, Newmarket Road
Bury St Edmunds, Suffolk, IP33 3YB
Email: info@halleonardeurope.com

In Australia contact:
Hal Leonard Australia Pty. Ltd.
4 Lentara Court
Cheltenham, Victoria, 3192 Australia
Email: info@halleonard.com.au

Contents

4   **FEEL IT STILL** *Portugal. The Man*

16   **LOST IN JAPAN** *Shawn Mendes*

11   **THE MIDDLE** *Zedd, Maren Morris, Grey*

20   **REWRITE THE STARS** *from* THE GREATEST SHOWMAN

28   **WHATEVER IT TAKES** *Imagine Dragons*

FEEL IT STILL

Words and Music by JOHN GOURLEY, ZACH CAROTHERS,
JASON SECHRIST, ERIC HOWK, KYLE O'QUIN,
BRIAN HOLLAND, FREDDIE GORMAN, GEORGIA DOBBINS,
ROBERT BATEMAN, WILLIAM GARRETT, JOHN HILL
and ASA TACCONE

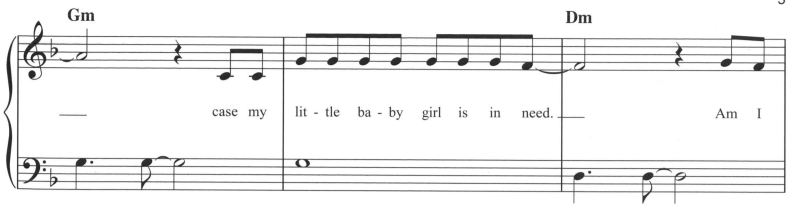

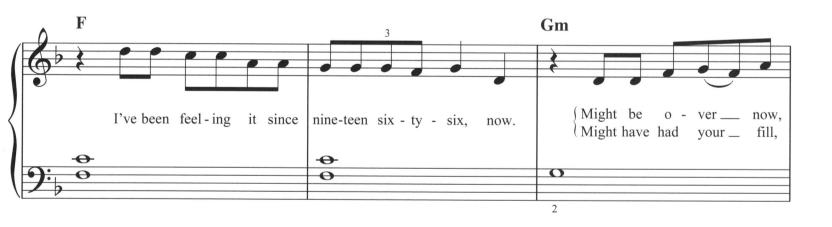

reb - el just for kicks, now. Let me kick it like it's nine-teen eight - y - six, now.

Might be o - ver ___ now, but I feel it still.

Got an - oth - er mouth to feed. ___

Leave it with a ba - by - sit - ter; Ma - ma, call the grave - dig - ger.

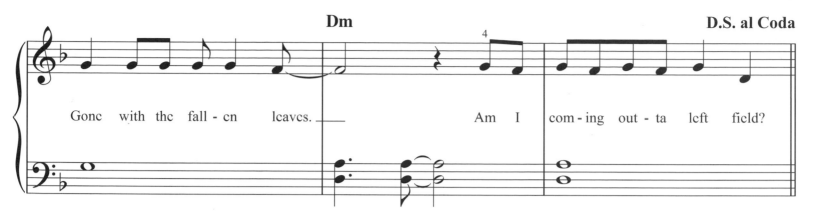

Dm   **D.S. al Coda**

Gone with the fall - en leaves. Am I com - ing out - ta left field?

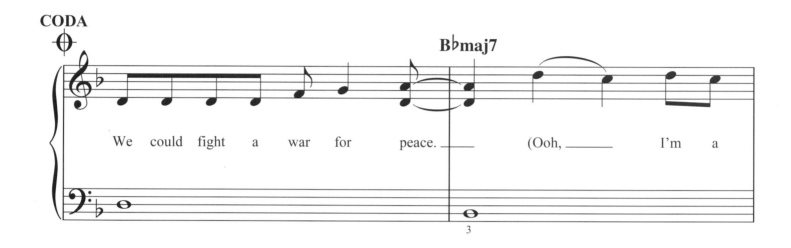

CODA   **B♭maj7**

We could fight a war for peace. (Ooh, I'm a

Gm   **Dm**

reb - el just for kicks, now.) Give in to that eas - y liv - ing; good-bye to my hopes and dreams,

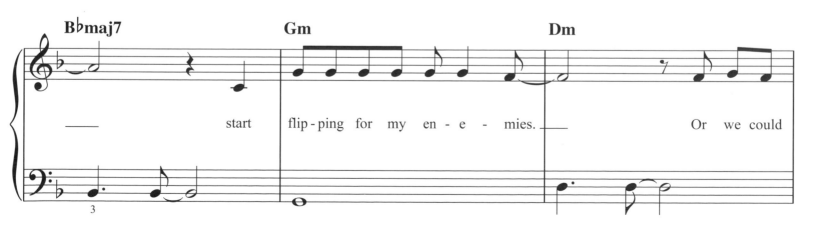

B♭maj7   **Gm**   **Dm**

start flip - ping for my en - e - mies. Or we could

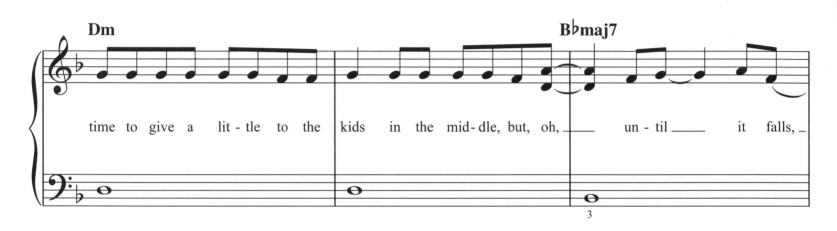

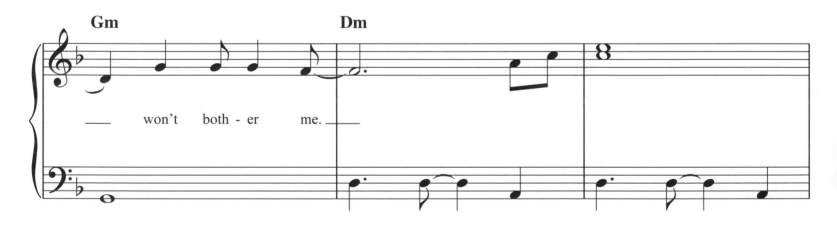

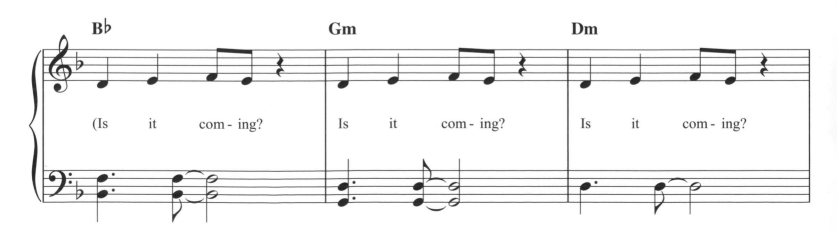

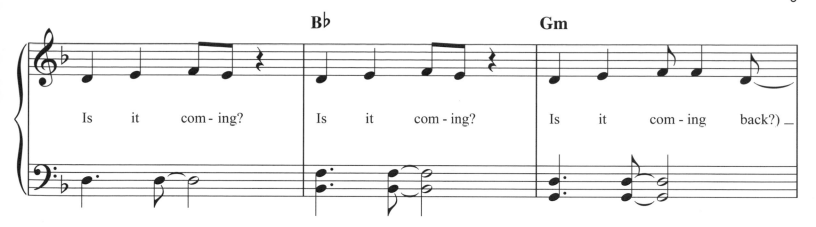

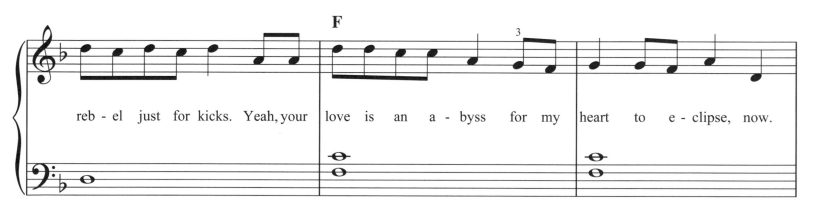

Ooh, _____ I'm a reb - el just for kicks, now.

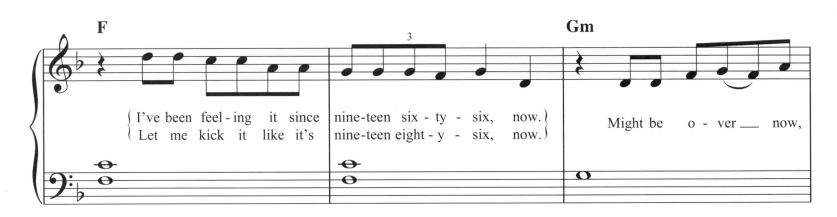

F

I've been feel-ing it since | nine-teen six - ty - six, now.
Let me kick it like it's | nine-teen eight - y - six, now.

Gm

Might be o - ver _____ now,

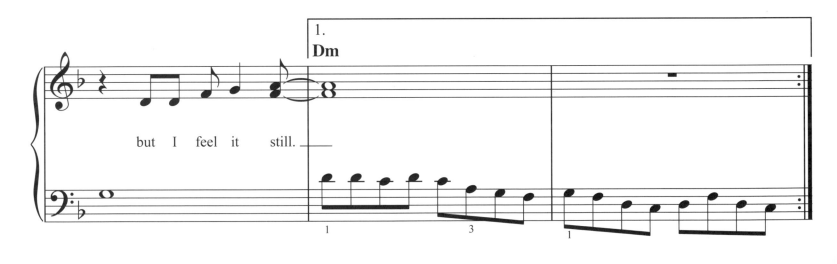

1.
Dm

but I feel it still. _____

2.
Dm

_____ Might have had your fill, but you feel it still. _____

THE MIDDLE

Words and Music by SARAH AARONS,
MARCUS LOMAX, JORDAN JOHNSON,
ANTON ZASLAVSKI, KYLE TREWARTHA,
MICHAEL TREWARTHA and STEFAN JOHNSON

Moderately fast

ba - by,   why don't you just meet me in the   mid - dle?   I'm

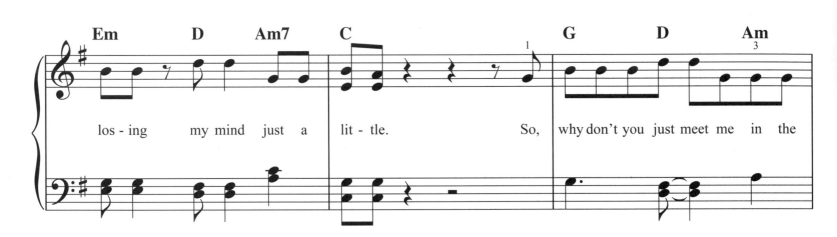

los - ing   my mind just a   lit - tle.   So,   why don't you just meet me in the

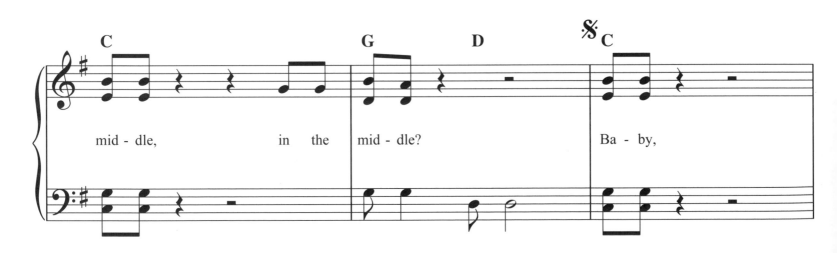

mid - dle,   in the   mid - dle?   Ba - by,

why don't you just meet me in the   mid - dle?   I'm   los - ing   my mind just a

lit - tle.　　So,　why don't you just meet me　in the　mid - dle,　　　in the

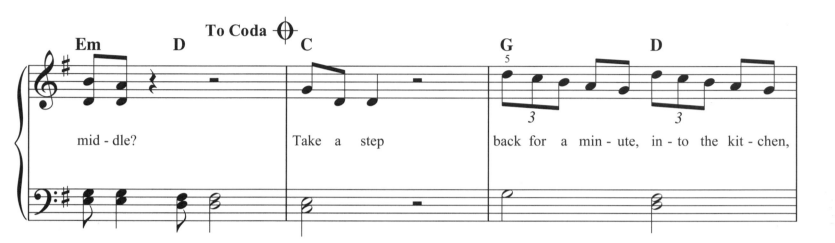

mid - dle?　　Take a step　　back for a min - ute, in - to the kit - chen,

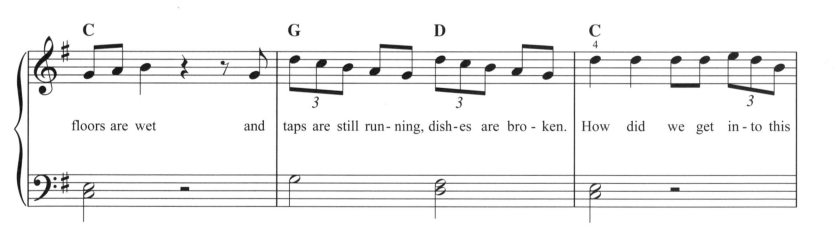

floors are wet　　and　taps are still run - ning, dish - es are bro - ken.　How did　we get in - to this

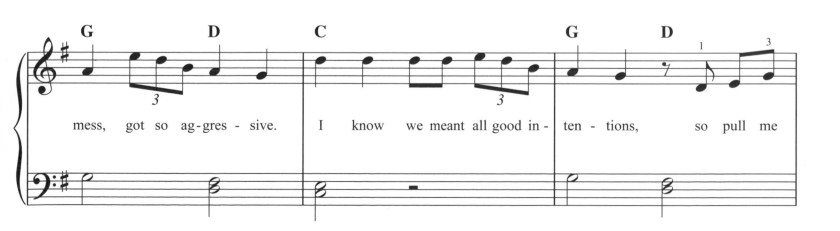

mess,　got so ag - gres - sive.　I　know　we meant all good in - ten - tions,　so pull me

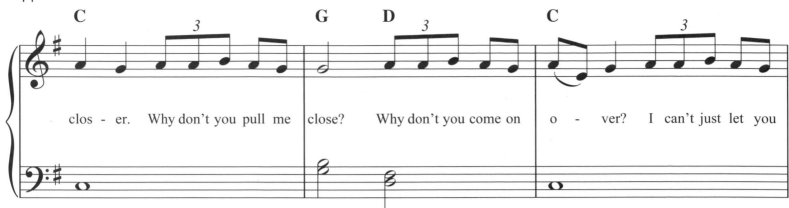

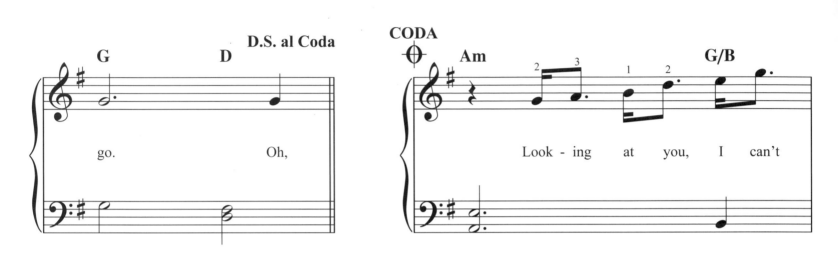

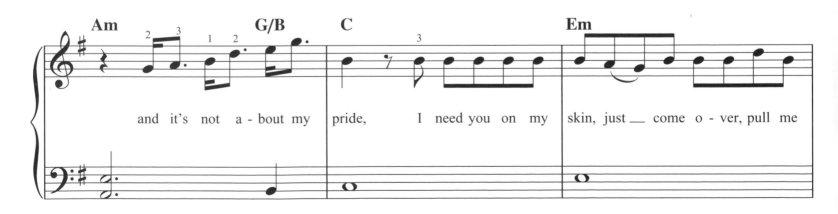

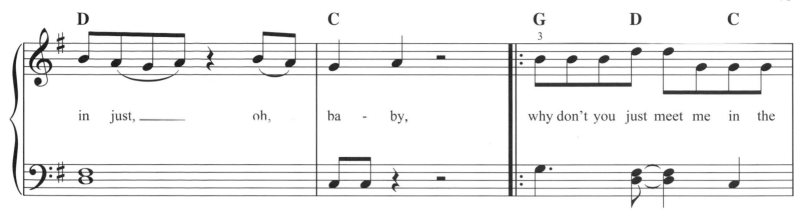

LOST IN JAPAN

Words and Music by SHAWN MENDES,
TEDDY GEIGER, SCOTT HARRIS
and NATE MERCEREAU

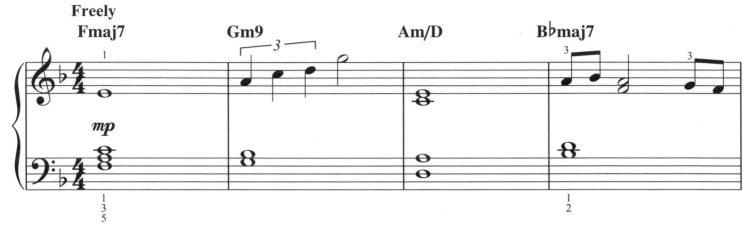

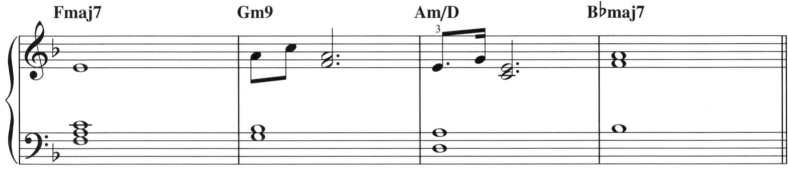

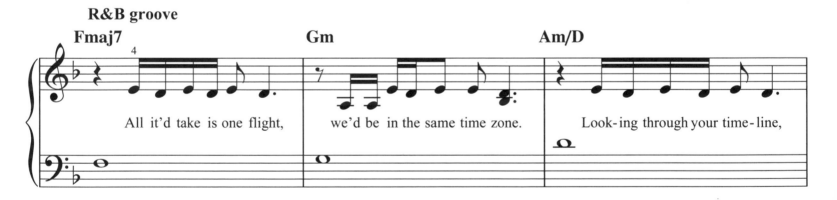

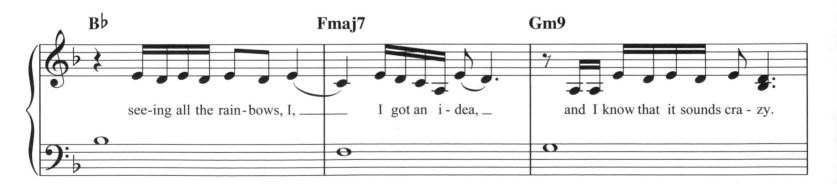

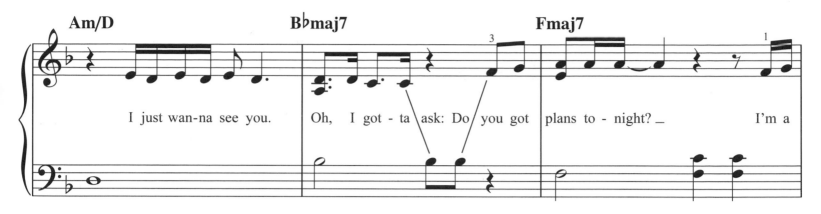

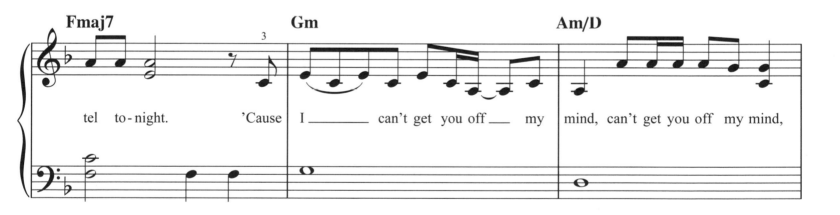

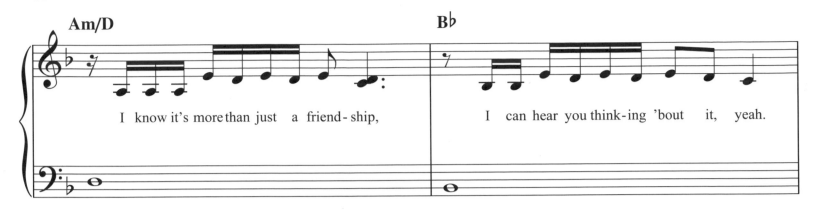

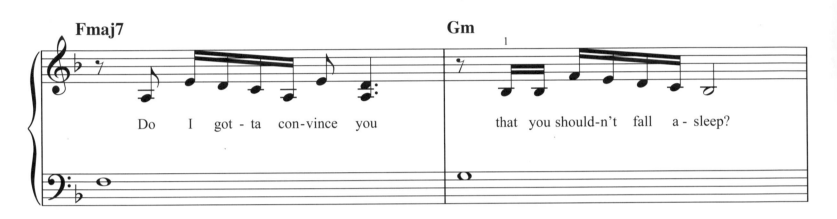

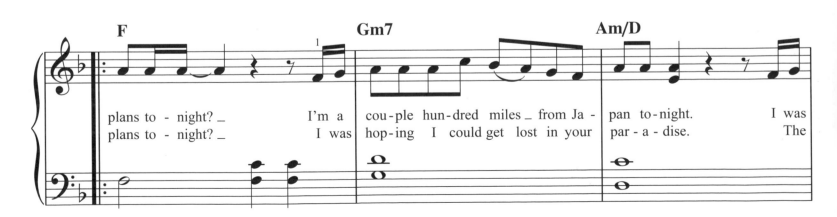

Bbmaj7 / Fmaj7 / Gm

think-ing I could fly to your ho- / tel to-night. / 'Cause I _____ can't get you off ____ my
on - ly thing I'm think-ing 'bout is / you and I. / 'Cause I _____ can't get you off ____ my

Am/D / Bbmaj7 Am7 Gm7 (1.)

mind, can't get you off my mind, / can't get you off my mind. Do you got
mind, can't get you off my mind,

2. Bbmaj7 Am7 Gm Bb/C / Fmaj7 / Gm7

I can't seem to get you off my / mind. Let's get lost to-night, ____ let's get lost to-night. __

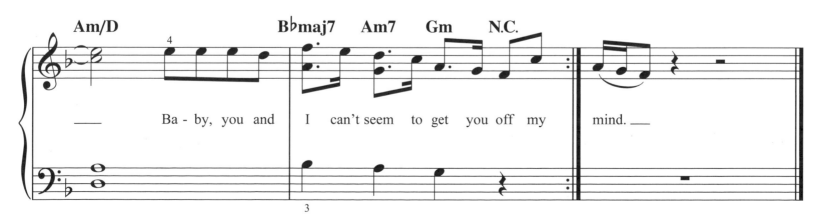

Am/D / Bbmaj7 Am7 Gm N.C.

__ Ba - by, you and / I can't seem to get you off my / mind. __

REWRITE THE STARS
from THE GREATEST SHOWMAN

Words and Music by BENJ PASEK
and JUSTIN PAUL

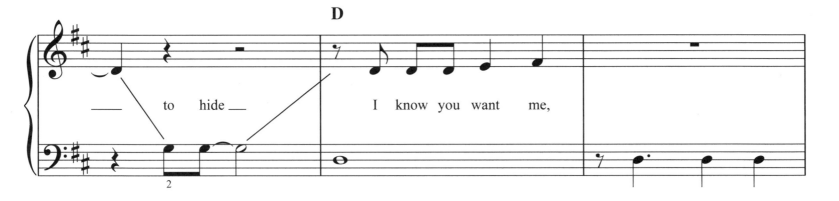

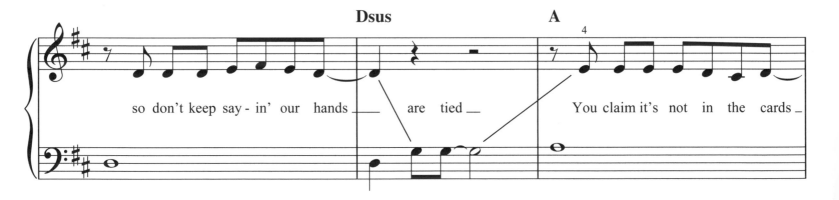

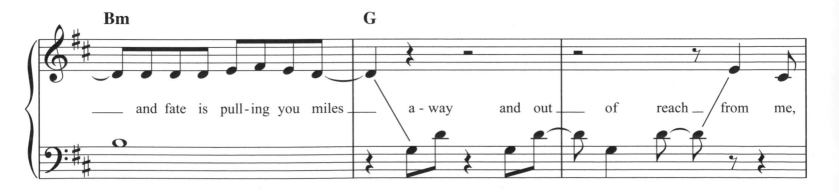

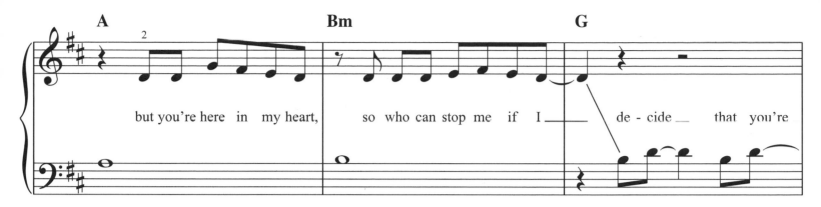

but you're here in my heart, so who can stop me if I _____ de - cide ____ that you're

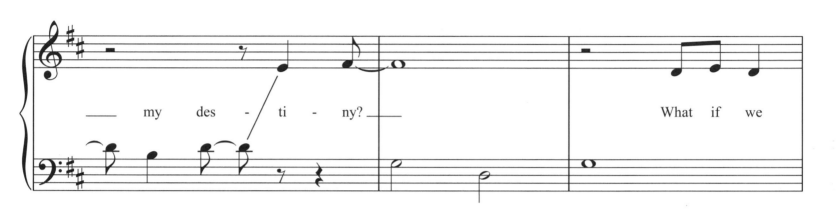

____ my des - ti - ny? ____ What if we

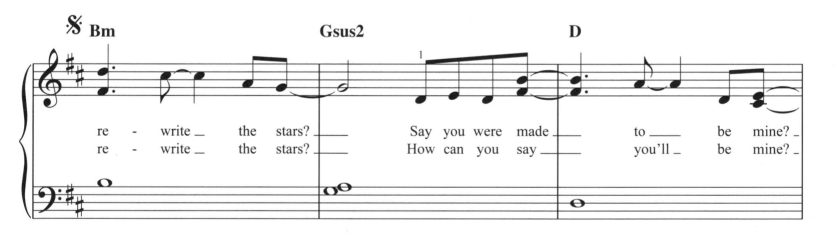

re - write ____ the stars? ____ Say you were made ____ to ____ be mine? _
re - write ____ the stars? ____ How can you say ____ you'll _ be mine? _

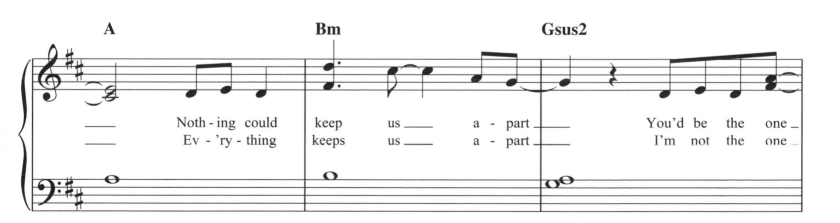

____ Noth - ing could keep us ____ a - part ____ You'd be the one _
____ Ev - 'ry - thing keeps us ____ a - part ____ I'm not the one _

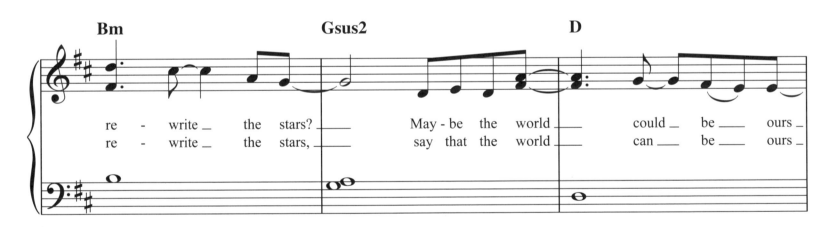

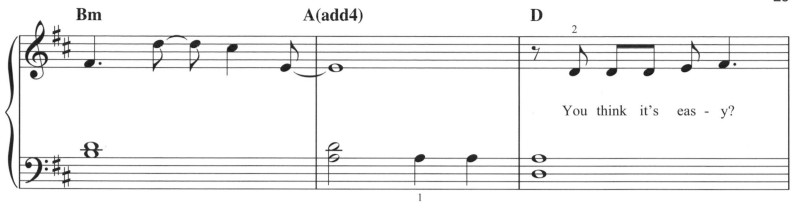

You think it's eas-y?

You think I don't want to run ____ to you? ____

But there are moun-tains, _____ and there are doors that we can't ____

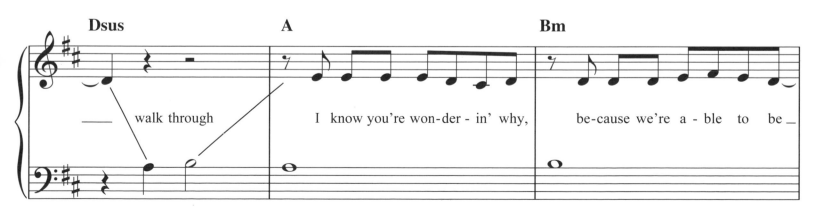

____ walk through I know you're won-der-in' why, be-cause we're a-ble to be ____

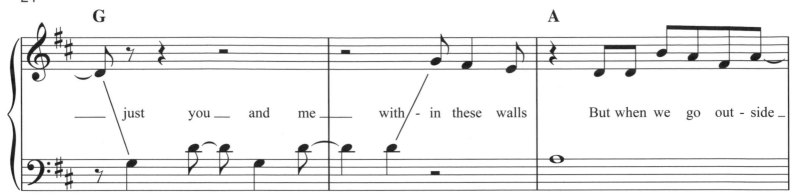

just you and me ___ with - in these walls   But when we go out - side ___

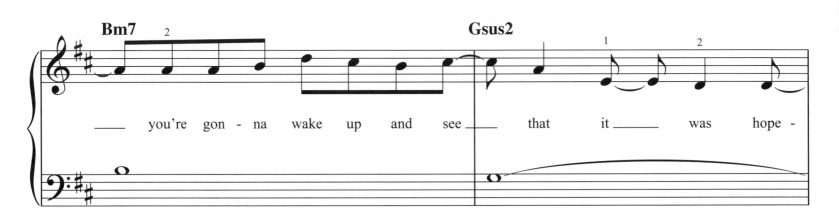

___ you're gon - na wake up and see ___ that it ___ was hope -

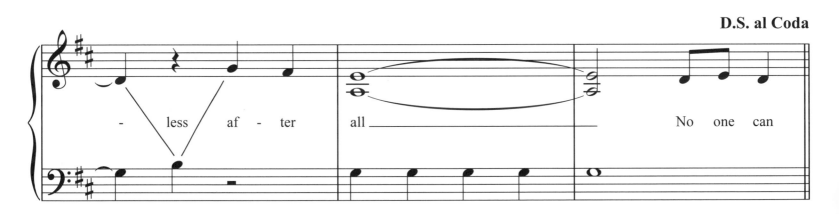

- less af - ter all ___   No one can

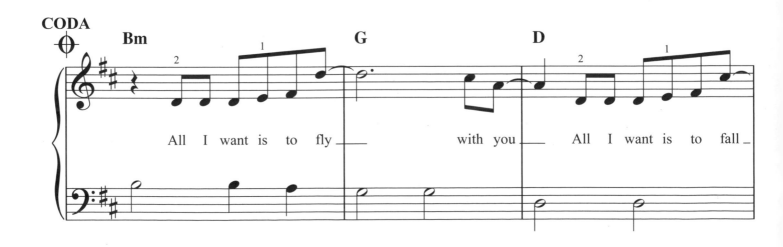

All I want is to fly ___ with you ___   All I want is to fall ___

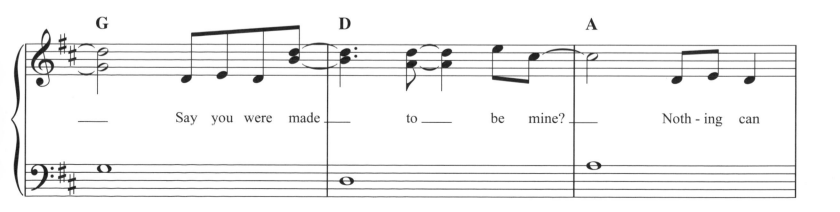

Bm · **G** · **D**

keep us ___ a - part ___ 'cause you are the one ___ I was meant ___ to find ___

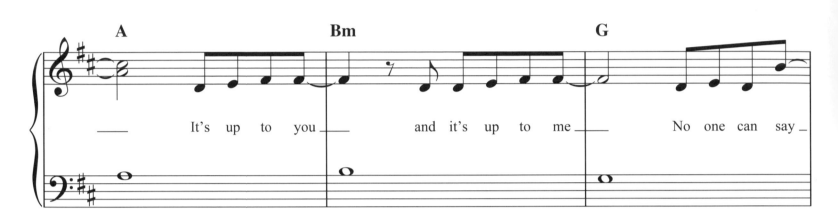

A · **Bm** · **G**

___ It's up to you ___ and it's up to me ___ No one can say ___

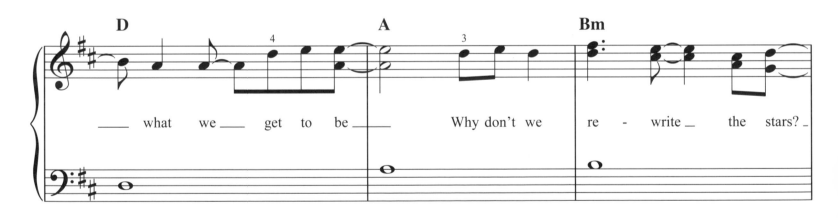

D · **A** · **Bm**

___ what we ___ get to be ___ Why don't we re - write ___ the stars? ___

G · **D** · **A**

___ chang - in' the world ___ to ___ be ours? ___

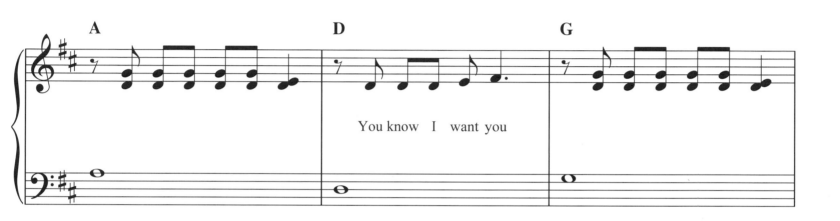

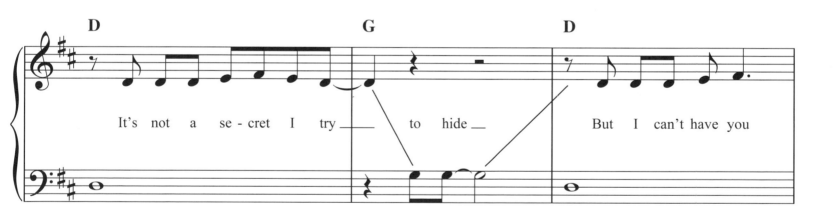

WHATEVER IT TAKES

Words and Music by DAN REYNOLDS,
WAYNE SERMON, BEN McKEE,
DANIEL PLATZMAN and JOEL LITTLE

Half-time Pop beat

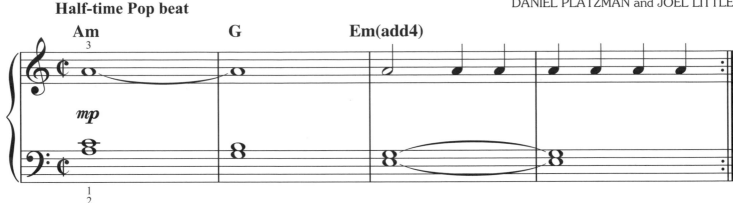

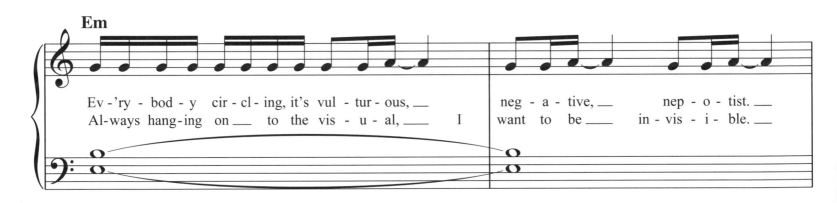

Fall-ing too fast to pre-pare for this, __ trip-ping in the world could be dan-ger-ous. __
Al-ways had a fear of be-ing ty-pi-cal, __ look-ing at my bod-y, feel-ing mis-'ra-ble. __

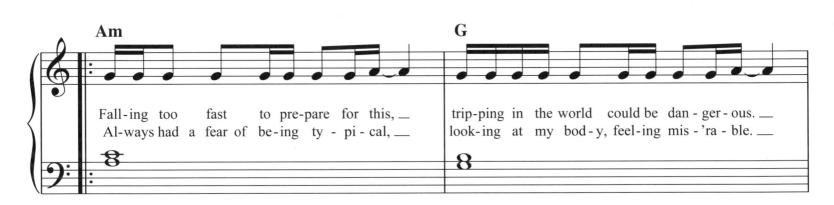

Ev-'ry-bod-y cir-cl-ing, it's vul-tur-ous, __ neg-a-tive, __ nep-o-tist. __
Al-ways hang-ing on __ to the vis-u-al, __ I want to be __ in-vis-i-ble. __

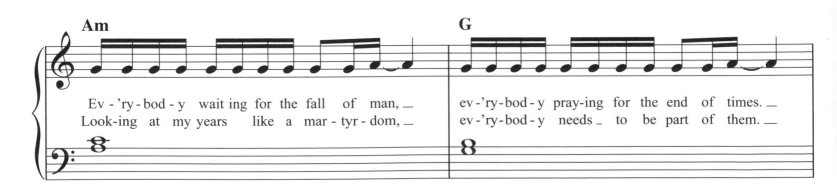

Ev-'ry-bod-y wait-ing for the fall of man, __ ev-'ry-bod-y pray-ing for the end of times. __
Look-ing at my years like a mar-tyr-dom, __ ev-'ry-bod-y needs __ to be part of them. __

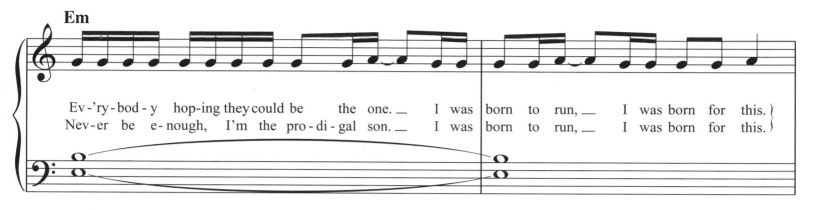

Ev-'ry-bod-y hop-ing they could be the one. __ I was born to run, __ I was born for this.
Nev-er be e-nough, I'm the pro-di-gal son. __ I was born to run, __ I was born for this.

Whip, whip, run me like a race horse. Pull me like a rip - cord, break me down and

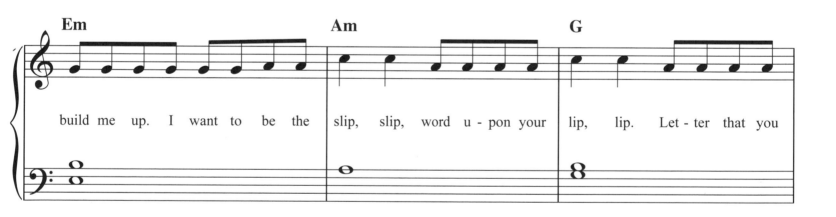

build me up. I want to be the slip, slip, word u - pon your lip, lip. Let - ter that you

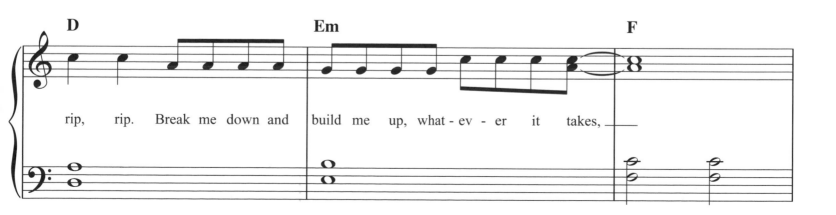

rip, rip. Break me down and build me up, what - ev - er it takes, __

30

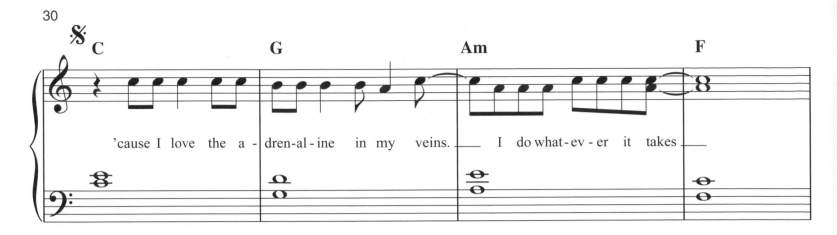

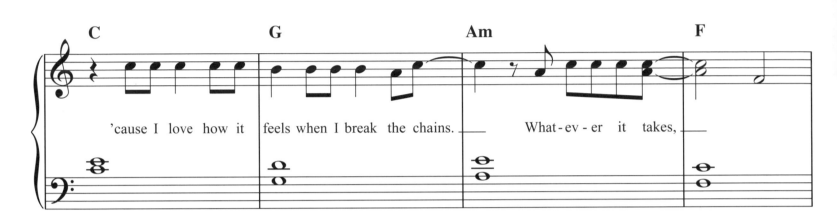

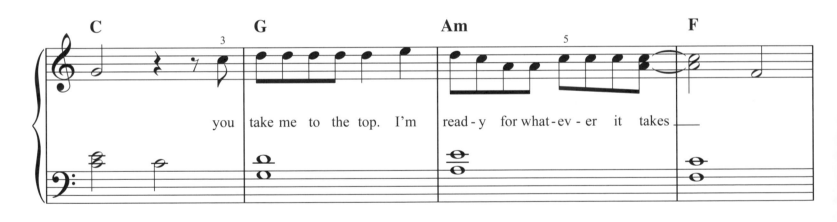

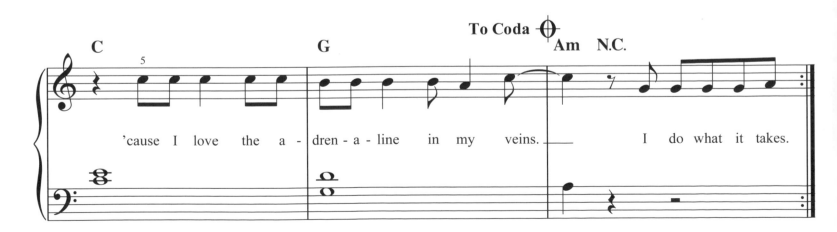

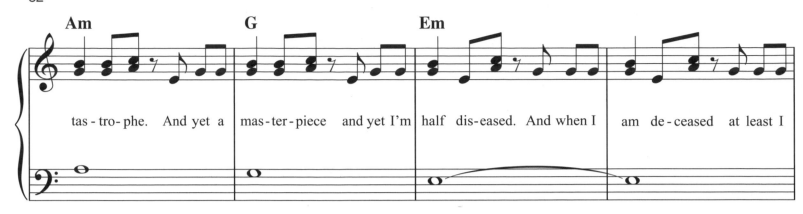

tas-tro-phe. And yet a | mas-ter-piece and yet I'm | half dis-eased. And when I | am de-ceased at least I

go down to the grave and die | hap-pi-ly. Leave the | bod-y of my soul to be a

part of me. | I do what it takes.

D.S. al Coda

CODA

What-ev-er it takes

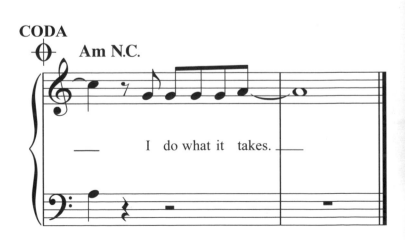

I do what it takes.